Dig Deep in Scripture Series

PRAYING WITH PAUL

BIBLE STUDY JOURNAL

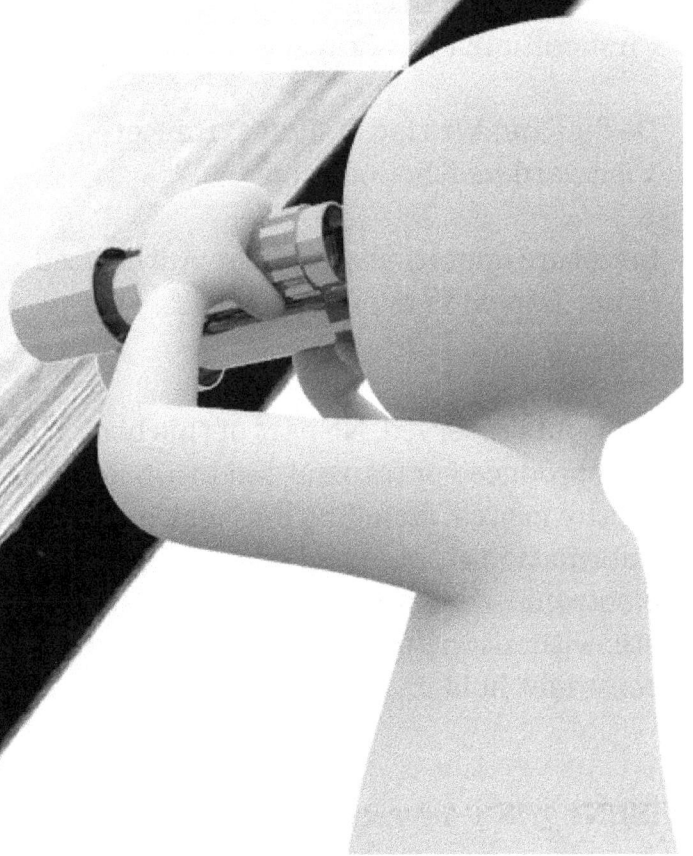

BY JAX

Published by Battle Road Books in 2016
First edition; First Printing

Design and Writing © Jax M. Hunter
VisitGardenoftheGods.com

Scripture quotations from The Authorized
(King James) Version (KJV)

Battle Road Books

ISBN# 978-1-945922-01-5

Dedication

To Judi, who many years ago brought the story of Gideon to life by digging deep into the meaning of the words.

Who am I? I'm not a bible scholar, but I love the Word of God. Just like you. Someone who is seeking to do better. To do it His way.

We don't need special training to look for hidden treasures in the Word.

What did Jesus say about the Spirit?   Howbeit when he, the Spirit of truth, is come, he will guide you into all truth (John 16:13 KJV)   The Greek word for that advocate is *paracletos* - one who comes along side you to help, teach, counsel and strengthen you. Cool word.

This journal is a 16-week journey through the four main prayers of Paul in his letters to the Ephesians, the Philippians and the Colossians. It is my hope that, in these prayers, you'll find an amazing call to prayer in your own life – to pray these prayers for yourself and for others.

There will be small "assignments" each day, not too big that you'll have to set aside large chunks of time to do them. And there is plenty of room in this book for you to write out the insights you gather along the way. Maybe even room to come back to these scriptures and have another look at them when you're done. I am creating this journal and the others in the series for me too. I'll be the first one to order. My intention is to go through it over and over – maybe use a different color ink for each time through. I'm smiling as I type this.

Looking forward to this adventure.

Enjoy this book. Don't stress over the work. Some of you will find new tools to better understand Scripture. Some of you are familiar with the tools but maybe haven't used them in a while. Whatever you give to this study will be given back to you good measure, pressed down, shaken together, and running over.

Jax

Diggin' Deep into Scripture

In this journal/workbook we will be going on a retreat to dig for hidden treasure. We'll be camping out (so we don't have to waste time traveling) very near where our map shows hidden treasure.

We'll pitch our tents and make ready our campfires.

Imagine it. We'll get up with the sun and start our day with prayer.

We'll ask the Father for guidance by his Spirit to dig deep in to the Word to find awesome treasures in the prayers of Paul. We'll have a hearty breakfast and, as the sun begins to warm us, we'll be able to take off our jackets.

Then we'll heft our backpacks and grab our picks and shovels for our day's adventure. We'll follow the trails through the wild, checking our map, and shortly come to where X marks the spot. Here, we'll explore the scriptures to excavate the treasures the Lord has for us.

As the sun sets, we'll make our way back to camp, encouraged that our hard work will pay off in ways we may never understand. Around the campfire, we'll stretch out, maybe roast a marshmallow or two and ponder the gems we've discovered today. With the stars in abundance overhead, we'll sing praise to the Lord for this wonderful world he's given us and his marvelous Word.

Then we'll enjoy the peaceful silence in our tents as we drift off to sleep, knowing that more adventure awaits us tomorrow.

Section One

Ephesians 1:17-19   (KJV)

17 That the God of our Lord Jesus Christ, the Father of glory, may give unto you the spirit of wisdom and revelation in the knowledge of him:

18 The eyes of your understanding being enlightened; that ye may know what is the hope of his calling, and what the riches of the glory of his inheritance in the saints,

19 And what is the exceeding greatness of his power to us-ward who believe, according to the working of his mighty power . . .

Week One

Ephesians 1:17   (KJV)

17 That the God of our Lord Jesus Christ, the Father of glory, may give unto you the spirit of wisdom and revelation in the knowledge of him:

Day 1

Read the section in context – the entire chapter.

Look up other versions online and write out the one that you love the best. Here's a link for that: (https://www.blueletterbible.org)

Days 2&3

Look up the words in a Greek Lexicon (http://www.eliyah.com/lexicon.html)

I've **bolded** the ones that might hold amazing treasures. (Not that you're limited by my boldness.) :)

What treasures did you find? Did looking up these words make any difference in how you interpret the verses? Journal your thoughts.

Eph 1:17 That the God of our Lord Jesus Christ, the Father of glory, may give unto you the **spirit** of **wisdom** and **revelation** in the **knowledge** of him:

Day 4

Write out the entire prayer. (You can do this daily for memorization.)

Did you come upon any other scriptures that relate to this week's section of Paul's prayer?

Now that you've looked up all the words and maybe some linked scriptures, feel free to check out some commentaries that you can find on the Blue Letter Bible site or elsewhere.

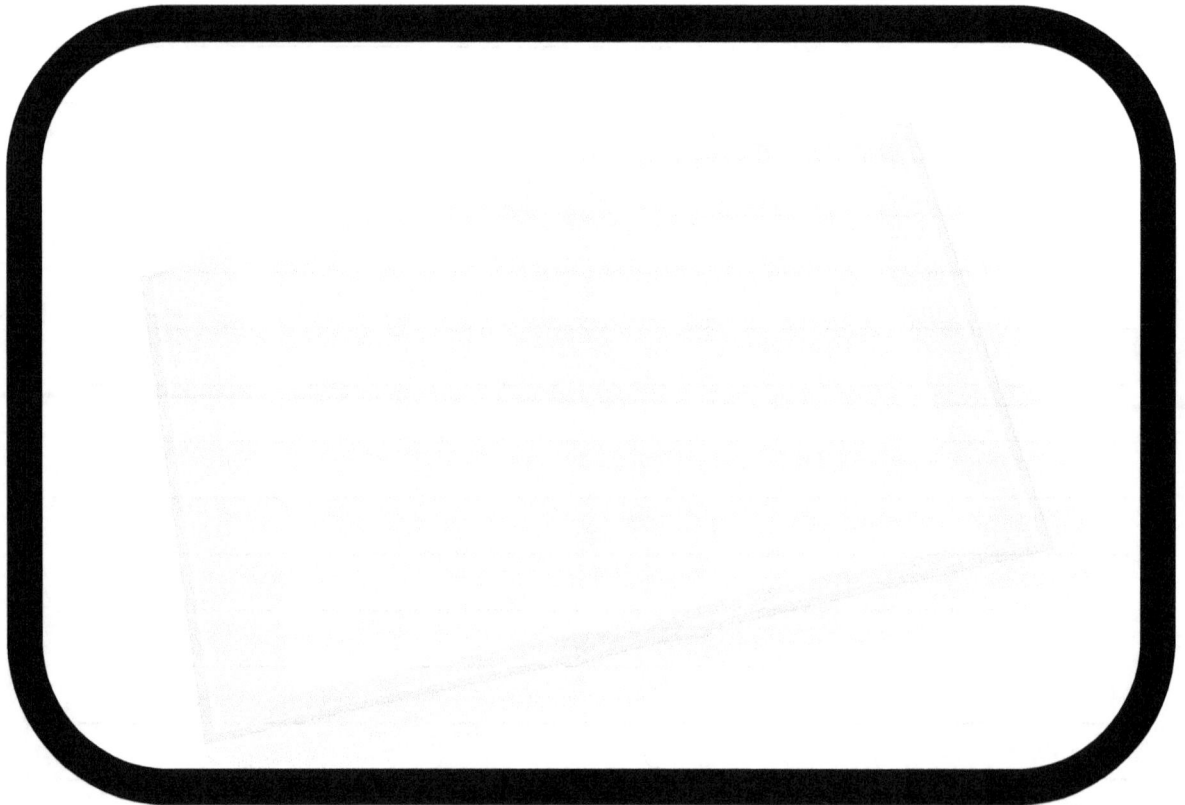

Day 5

Around the campfire – as you listen to the crackling fire, and stretch out, and look up at the milky way visible in the cloudless sky, ponder the treasures you've found today.

Journal your thoughts.

Day 6

Write out the section again making it personal – either for you or for someone you're praying for.

Expand on the section with insights you've gathered from your treasure hunt this week.

Week Two

Ephesians 1:18   (KJV)

18 The eyes of your understanding being enlightened; that ye may know what is the hope of his calling, and what the riches of the glory of his inheritance in the saints,

Day 1

Read the section in context – the entire chapter.

Look up other versions online and write out the one that you love the best. Here's a link for that: (https://www.blueletterbible.org)

Days 2&3

Look up the words in a Greek Lexicon
(http://www.eliyah.com/lexicon.html)

I've **bolded** the ones that might hold amazing
treasures. (Not that you're limited by my
boldness.) :)

What treasures did you find? Did looking up
these words make any difference in how you
interpret the verses? Journal your thoughts.

Eph 1: 18 The eyes of your
understanding being **enlightened**;
that ye may **know** what is the **hope**
of his **calling**, and what the **riches** of
the **glory** of his **inheritance** in the
saints,

Day 4

Write out the entire prayer. (You can do this daily for memorization.)

Did you come upon any other scriptures that relate to this week's section of Paul's prayer?

Now that you've looked up all the words and maybe some linked scriptures, feel free to check out some commentaries that you can find on the Blue Letter Bible site or elsewhere.

Day 5

Around the campfire – as you listen to the crackling fire, and stretch out, and look up at the milky way visible in the cloudless sky, ponder the treasures you've found today.

Journal your thoughts.

Day 6

Write out the section again making it personal – either for you or for someone you're praying for.

Expand on the section with insights you've gathered from your treasure hunt this week.

Week Three

Ephesians 1:19a (KJV)

19 And what is the exceeding greatness of his power to us-ward who believe,

Day 1

Read the section in context – the entire chapter.

Look up other versions online and write out the one that you love the best. Here's a link for that: (https://www.blueletterbible.org)

Days 2&3

Look up the words in a Greek Lexicon (http://www.eliyah.com/lexicon.html)

I've **bolded** the ones that might hold amazing treasures. (Not that you're limited by my boldness.) :)

What treasures did you find? Did looking up these words make any difference in how you interpret the verses? Journal your thoughts.

Eph 1:19a And what is the **exceeding greatness** of his **power** to us-ward who **believe**,

Day 4

Write out the entire prayer. (You can do this daily for memorization.)

Did you come upon any other scriptures that relate to this week's section of Paul's prayer?

Now that you've looked up all the words and maybe some linked scriptures, feel free to check out some commentaries that you can find on the Blue Letter Bible site or elsewhere.

Day 5

Around the campfire – as you listen to the crackling fire, and stretch out, and look up at the milky way visible in the cloudless sky, ponder the treasures you've found today.

Journal your thoughts.

Day 6

Write out the section again making it personal –
either for you or for someone you're praying for.

Expand on the section with insights you've
gathered from your treasure hunt this week.

Week Four

Ephesians 1:19b   (KJV)

19b according to the working of his mighty power . . .

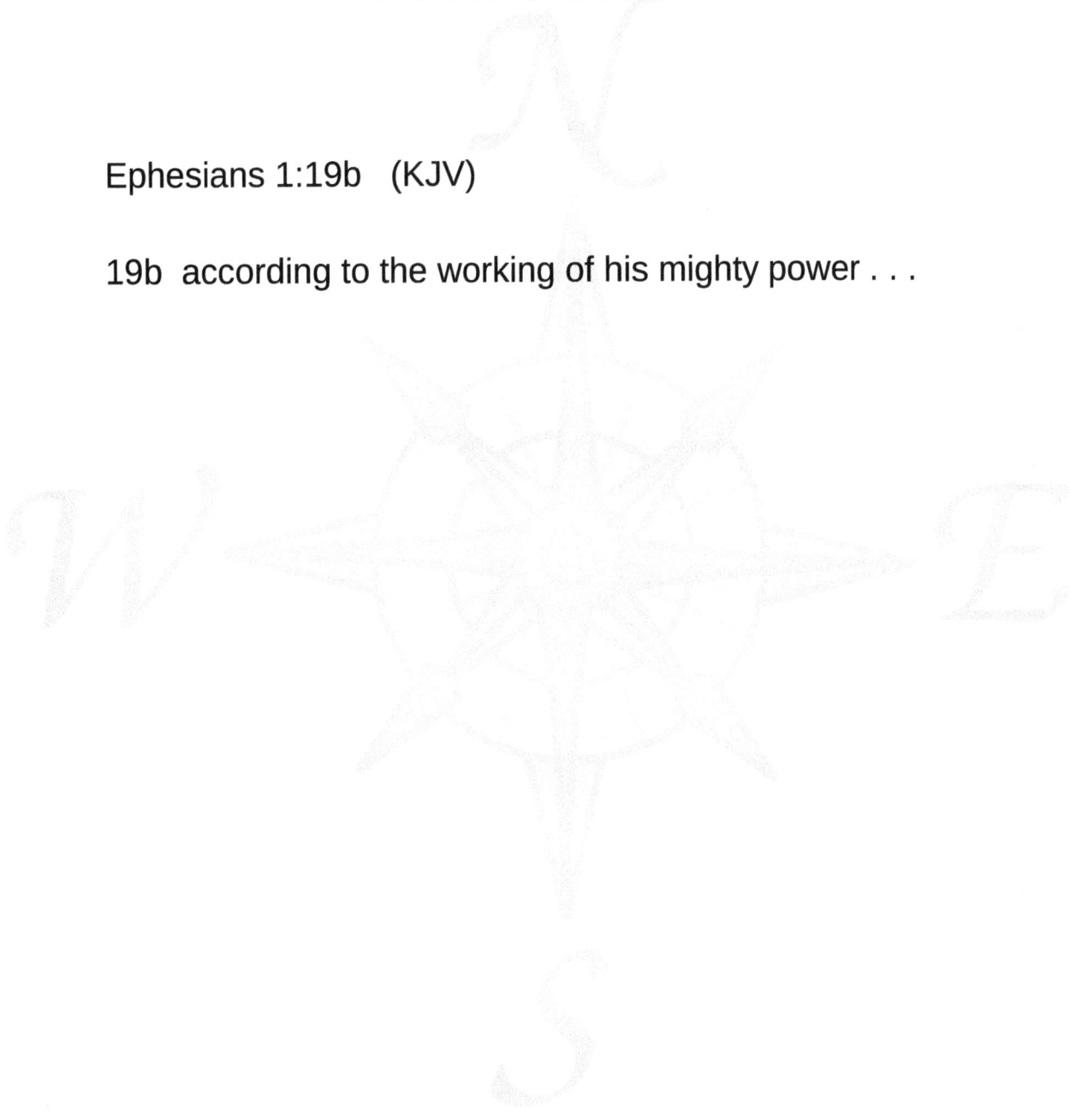

Day 1

Read the section in context – the entire chapter.
Look up other versions online and write out the one
that you love the best. Here's a link for that:
 (https://www.blueletterbible.org)

Days 2&3

Look up the words in a Greek Lexicon
(http://www.eliyah.com/lexicon.html)

I've **bolded** the ones that might hold amazing
treasures. (Not that you're limited by my
boldness.) :)

What treasures did you find? Did looking up
these words make any difference in how you
interpret the verses? Journal your thoughts.

Eph 1: 19b according to the **working**
of his **mighty power**

Day 4

Write out the entire prayer. (You can do this daily for memorization.)

Did you come upon any other scriptures that relate to this week's section of Paul's prayer?

Now that you've looked up all the words and maybe some linked scriptures, feel free to check out some commentaries that you can find on the Blue Letter Bible site or elsewhere.

Day 5

Around the campfire – as you listen to the crackling fire, and stretch out, and look up at the milky way visible in the cloudless sky, ponder the treasures you've found today.

Journal your thoughts.

Day 6

Write out the section again making it personal –
either for you or for someone you're praying for.

Expand on the section with insights you've
gathered from your treasure hunt this week.

Section Two

Ephesians 3:16-19   (KJV)

16 That he would grant you, according to the riches of his glory, to be strengthened with might by his Spirit in the inner man;

17 That Christ may dwell in your hearts by faith; that ye, being rooted and grounded in love,

18 May be able to comprehend with all saints what is the breadth, and length, and depth, and height;

19 And to know the love of Christ, which passeth knowledge, that ye might be filled with all the fulness of God.

Week One

Ephesians 3:16   (KJV)

16 That he would grant you, according to the riches of his glory, to be strengthened with might by his Spirit in the inner man;

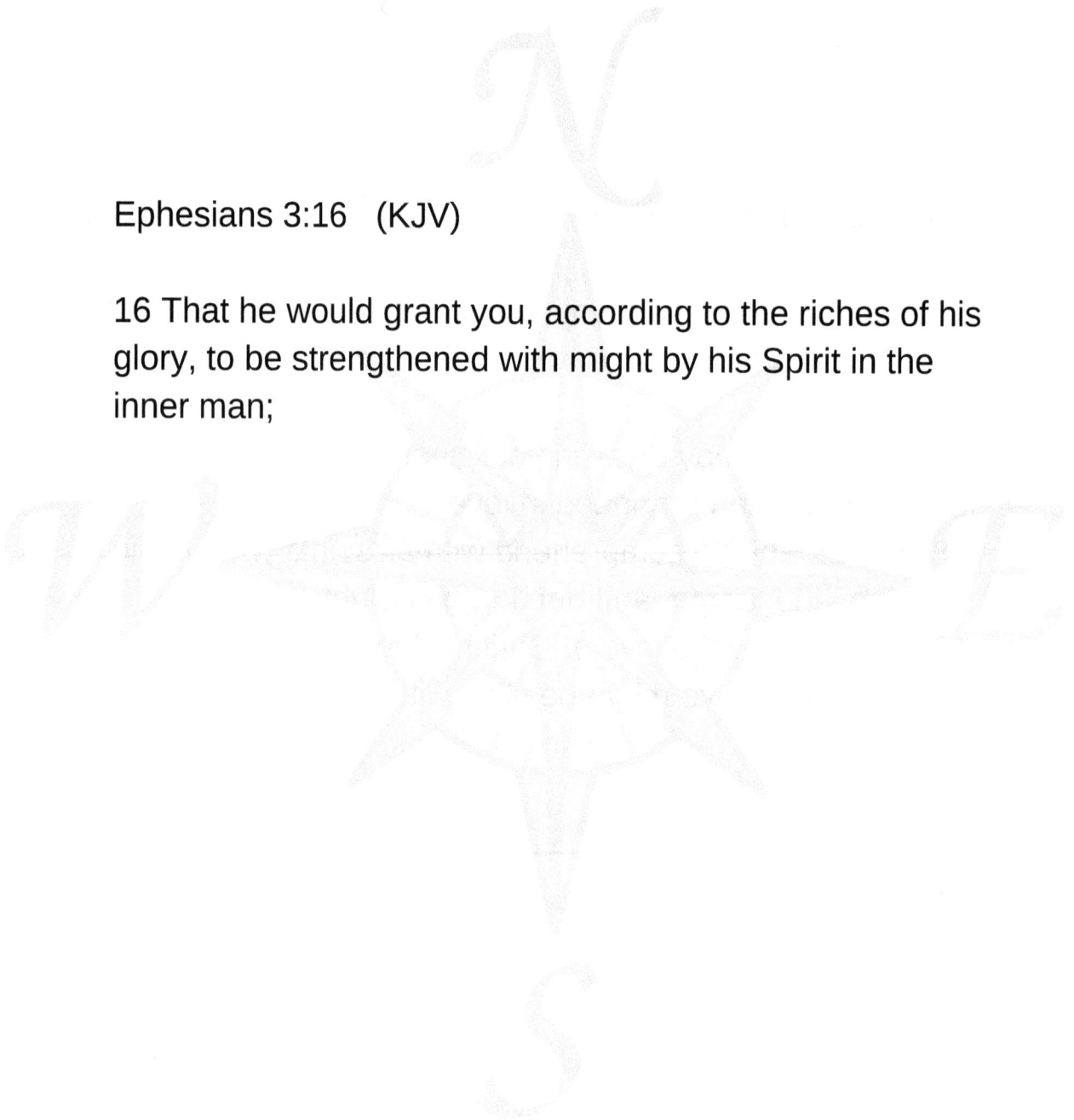

Day 1

Read the section in context – the entire chapter.

Look up other versions online and write out the one that you love the best. Here's a link for that: (https://www.blueletterbible.org)

Days 2&3

Look up the words in a Greek Lexicon (http://www.eliyah.com/lexicon.html)

I've **bolded** the ones that might hold amazing treasures. (Not that you're limited by my boldness.) :)

What treasures did you find? Did looking up these words make any difference in how you interpret the verses? Journal your thoughts.

Eph 3:16 That he would **grant** you, according to the **riches** of his **glory**, to be **strengthened** with **might** by his Spirit in the **inner** man;

Day 4

Write out the entire prayer. (You can do this daily for memorization.)

Did you come upon any other scriptures that relate to this week's section of Paul's prayer?

Now that you've looked up all the words and maybe some linked scriptures, feel free to check out some commentaries that you can find on the Blue Letter Bible site or elsewhere.

Day 5

Around the campfire – as you listen to the crackling fire, and stretch out, and look up at the milky way visible in the cloudless sky, ponder the treasures you've found today.

Journal your thoughts.

Day 6

Write out the section again making it personal – either for you or for someone you're praying for.

Expand on the section with insights you've gathered from your treasure hunt this week.

Week Two

Ephesians 3:17   (KJV)

17 That Christ may dwell in your hearts by faith; that ye, being rooted and grounded in love,

Day 1

Read the section in context – the entire chapter.

Look up other versions online and write out the one that you love the best. Here's a link for that: (https://www.blueletterbible.org)

Days 2&3

Look up the words in a Greek Lexicon (http://www.eliyah.com/lexicon.html)

I've **bolded** the ones that might hold amazing treasures. (Not that you're limited by my boldness.) :)

What treasures did you find? Did looking up these words make any difference in how you interpret the verses? Journal your thoughts.

> Eph 3: 17 That Christ may **dwell** in your **hearts** by **faith**; that ye, being **rooted** and **grounded** in **love**,

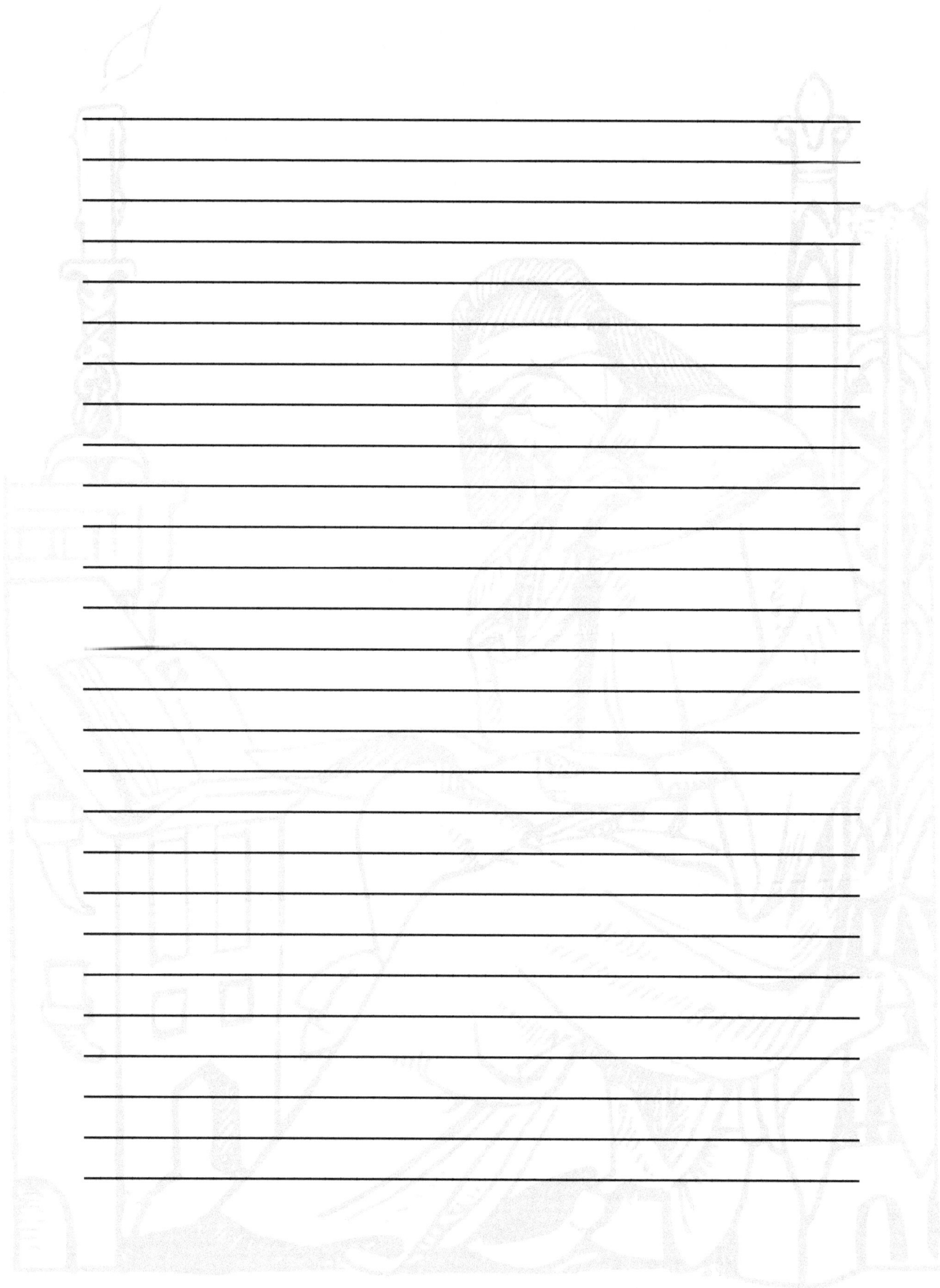

Day 4

Write out the entire prayer. (You can do this daily for memorization.)

Did you come upon any other scriptures that relate to this week's section of Paul's prayer?

Now that you've looked up all the words and maybe some linked scriptures, feel free to check out some commentaries that you can find on the Blue Letter Bible site or elsewhere.

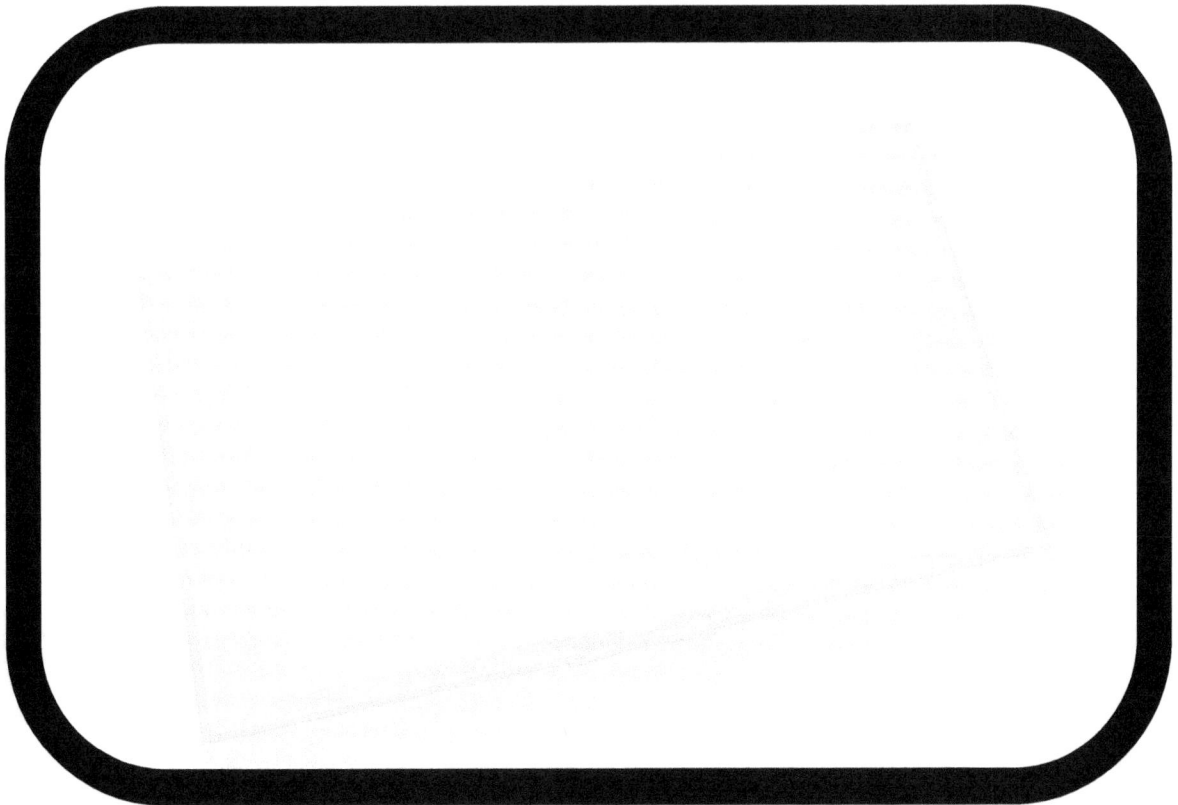

Day 5

Around the campfire – as you listen to the crackling fire, and stretch out, and look up at the milky way visible in the cloudless sky, ponder the treasures you've found today.

Journal your thoughts.

Day 6

Write out the section again making it personal – either for you or for someone you're praying for.

Expand on the section with insights you've gathered from your treasure hunt this week.

Week Three

Ephesians 3:18   (KJV)

18 May be able to comprehend with all saints what is the breadth, and length, and depth, and height;

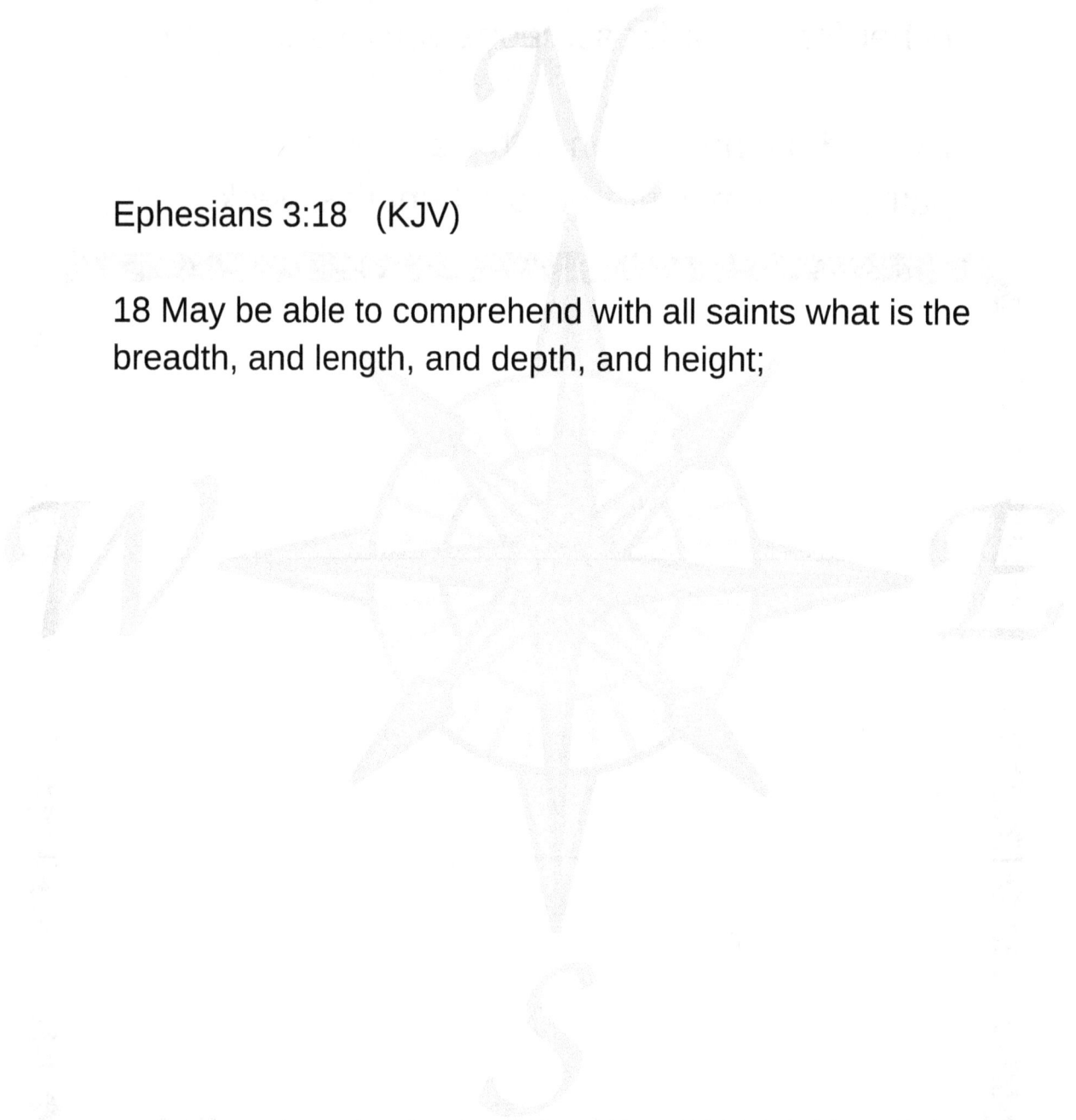

Day 1

Read the section in context – the entire chapter.

Look up other versions online and write out the one that you love the best. Here's a link for that: (https://www.blueletterbible.org)

Days 2&3

Look up the words in a Greek Lexicon
(http://www.eliyah.com/lexicon.html)

I've **bolded** the ones that might hold amazing
treasures. (Not that you're limited by my
boldness.) :)

What treasures did you find? Did looking up
these words make any difference in how you
interpret the verses? Journal your thoughts.

Eph 3:18 May be able to
comprehend with all saints what is
the **breadth**, and **length**, and **depth**,
and **height**;

Day 4

Write out the entire prayer. (You can do this daily for memorization.)

Did you come upon any other scriptures that relate to this week's section of Paul's prayer?

Now that you've looked up all the words and maybe some linked scriptures, feel free to check out some commentaries that you can find on the Blue Letter Bible site or elsewhere.

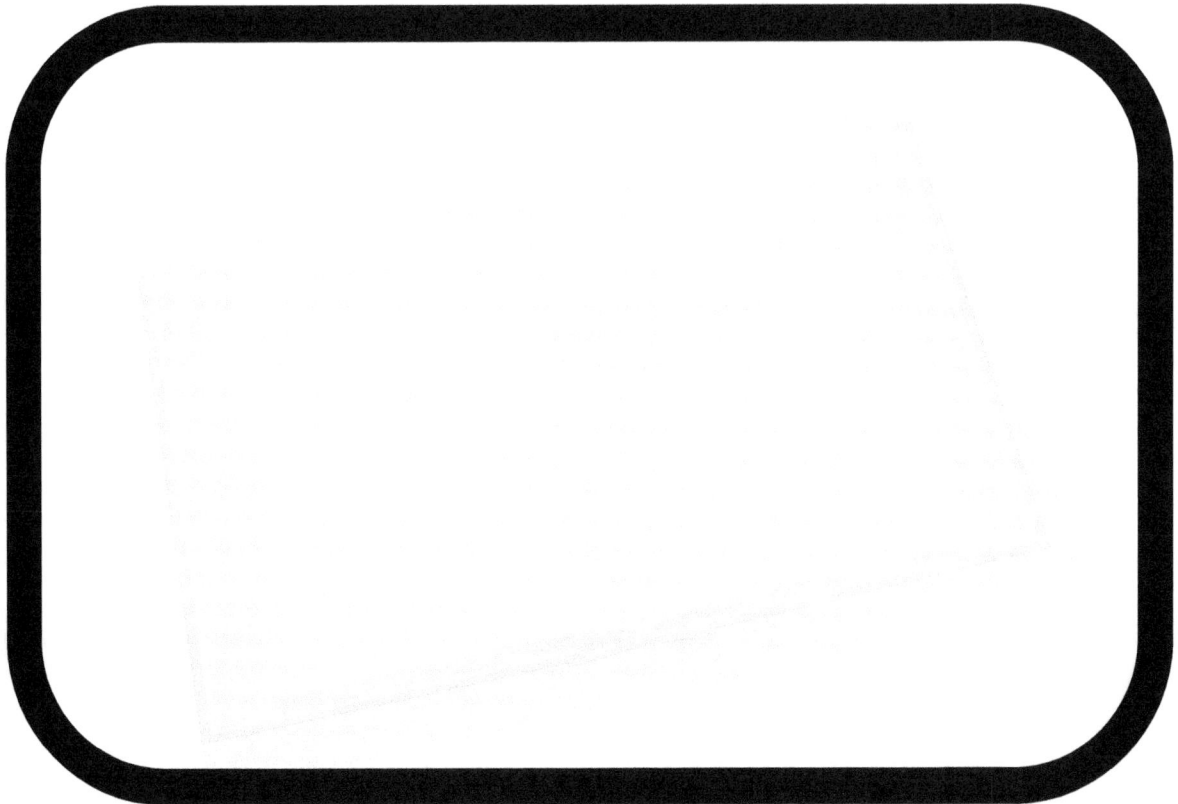

Day 5

Around the campfire – as you listen to the crackling fire, and stretch out, and look up at the milky way visible in the cloudless sky, ponder the treasures you've found today.

Journal your thoughts.

Day 6

Write out the section again making it personal –
either for you or for someone you're praying for.

Expand on the section with insights you've
gathered from your treasure hunt this week.

Week Four

Ephesians 3:19 (KJV)

19 And to know the love of Christ, which passeth knowledge, that ye might be filled with all the fulness of God.

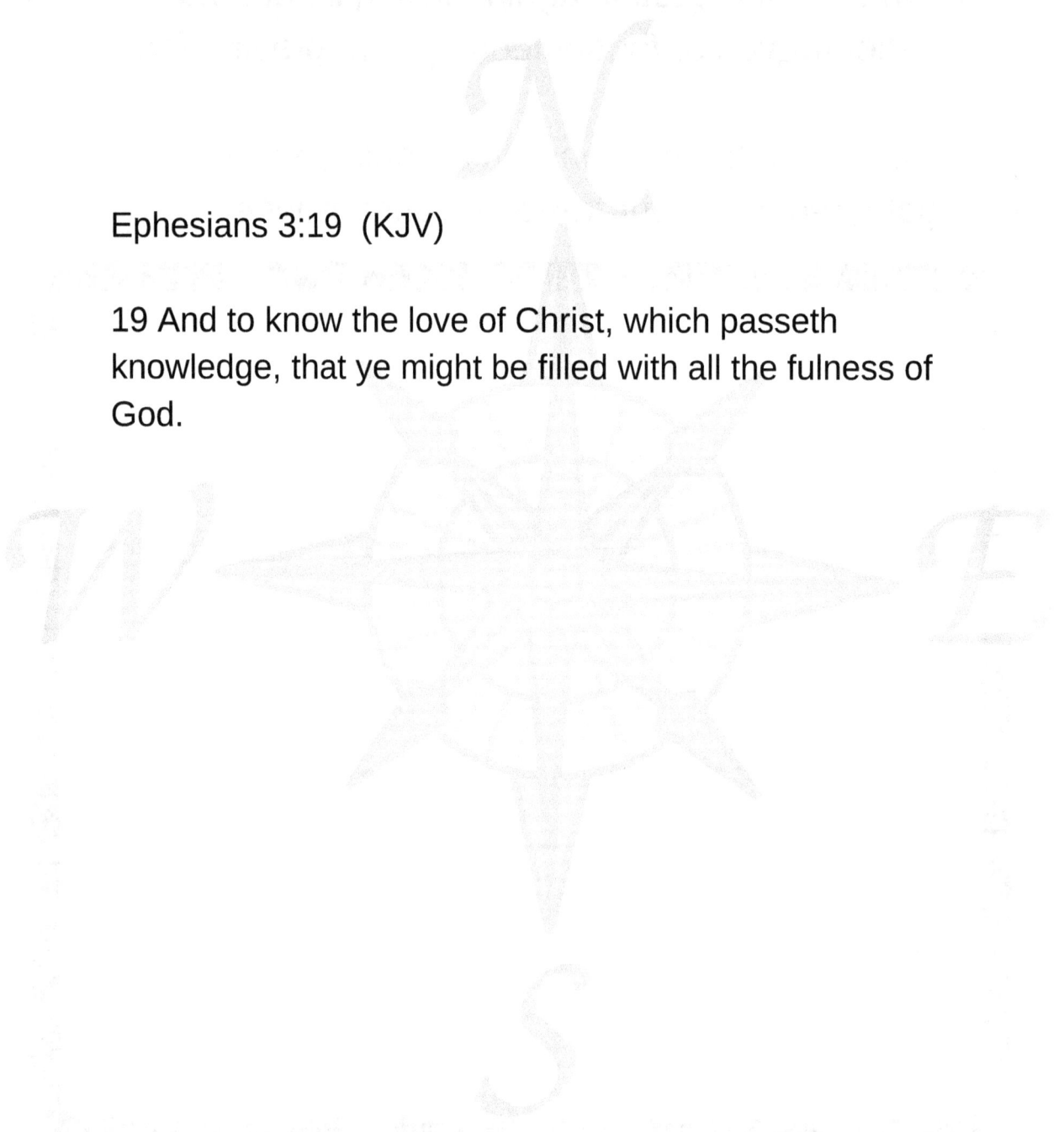

Day 1

Read the section in context – the entire chapter.

Look up other versions online and write out the one that you love the best. Here's a link for that: (https://www.blueletterbible.org)

Days 2&3

Look up the words in a Greek Lexicon
(http://www.eliyah.com/lexicon.html)

I've **bolded** the ones that might hold amazing
treasures. (Not that you're limited by my
boldness.) :)

What treasures did you find? Did looking up
these words make any difference in how you
interpret the verses? Journal your thoughts.

Eph 3:19 And to **know** the **love** of
Christ, which **passeth knowledge**,
that ye might be **filled** with all the
fulness of God.

Day 4

Write out the entire prayer. (You can do this daily for memorization.)

Did you come upon any other scriptures that relate to this week's section of Paul's prayer?

Now that you've looked up all the words and maybe some linked scriptures, feel free to check out some commentaries that you can find on the Blue Letter Bible site or elsewhere.

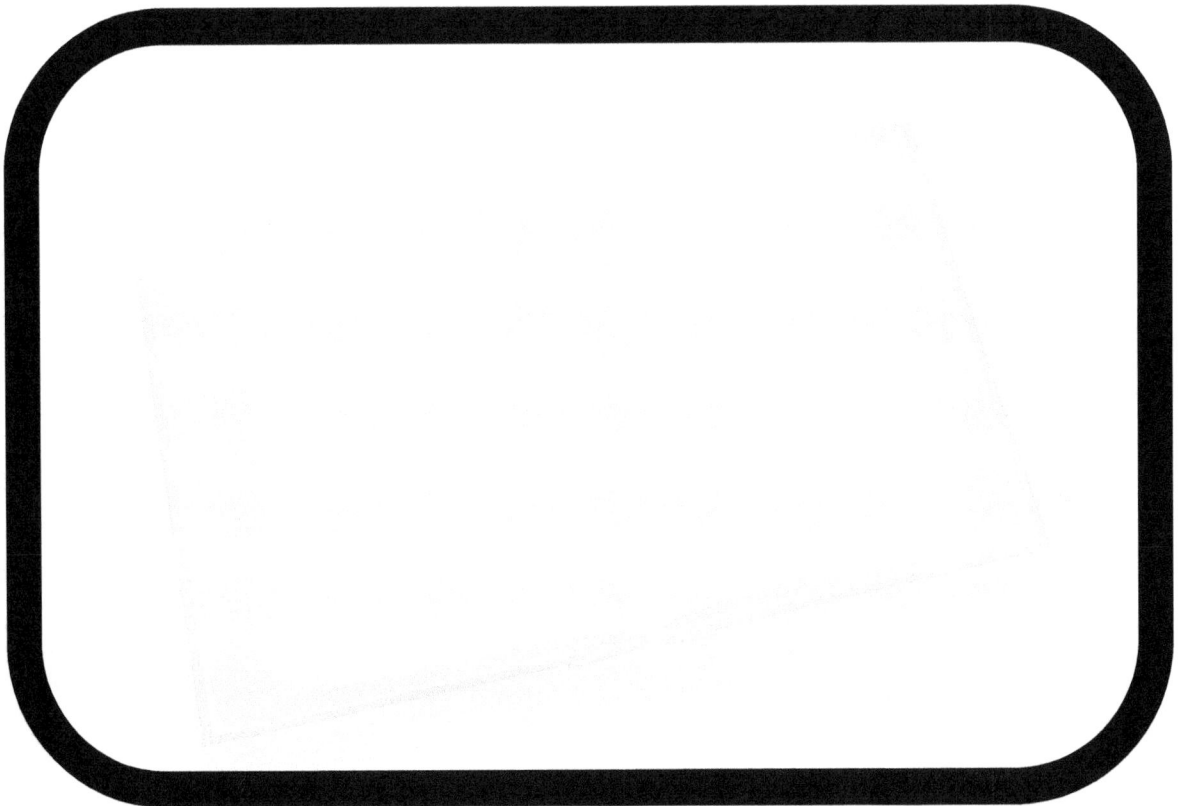

Day 5

Around the campfire – as you listen to the crackling fire, and stretch out, and look up at the milky way visible in the cloudless sky, ponder the treasures you've found today.

Journal your thoughts.

Day 6

Write out the section again making it personal – either for you or for someone you're praying for.

Expand on the section with insights you've gathered from your treasure hunt this week.

Section Three

Phil 1:9-11 (KJV)

9 And this I pray, that your love may abound yet more and more in knowledge and in all judgment;

10a That ye may approve things that are excellent;

10b that ye may be sincere and without offence till the day of Christ;

11 Being filled with the fruits of righteousness, which are by Jesus Christ, unto the glory and praise of God.

Week One

Phil 1:9 (KJV)

9 And this I pray, that your love may abound yet more and more in knowledge and in all judgment;

Day 1

Read the section in context – the entire chapter.

Look up other versions online and write out the one that you love the best. Here's a link for that: (https://www.blueletterbible.org)

Days 2&3

Look up the words in a Greek Lexicon (http://www.eliyah.com/lexicon.html)

I've **bolded** the ones that might hold amazing treasures. (Not that you're limited by my boldness.) :)

What treasures did you find? Did looking up these words make any difference in how you interpret the verses? Journal your thoughts.

Phil 1:9 And this I **pray**, that your **love** may **abound** yet **more and more** in **knowledge** and in all **judgment**;

Day 4

Write out the entire prayer. (You can do this daily for memorization.)

Did you come upon any other scriptures that relate to this week's section of Paul's prayer?

Now that you've looked up all the words and maybe some linked scriptures, feel free to check out some commentaries that you can find on the Blue Letter Bible site or elsewhere.

Day 5

Around the campfire – as you listen to the crackling fire, and stretch out, and look up at the milky way visible in the cloudless sky, ponder the treasures you've found today.

Journal your thoughts.

Day 6

Write out the section again making it personal – either for you or for someone you're praying for.

Expand on the section with insights you've gathered from your treasure hunt this week.

Week Two

Phil 1:10a (KJV)

10a That ye may approve things that are excellent;

Day 1

Read the section in context – the entire chapter.

Look up other versions online and write out the one that you love the best. Here's a link for that: (https://www.blueletterbible.org)

Days 2&3

Look up the words in a Greek Lexicon (http://www.eliyah.com/lexicon.html)

I've **bolded** the ones that might hold amazing treasures. (Not that you're limited by my boldness.) :)

What treasures did you find? Did looking up these words make any difference in how you interpret the verses? Journal your thoughts.

Phil 1:10a That ye may **approve** things that are **excellent**;

Day 4

Write out the entire prayer. (You can do this daily for memorization.)

Did you come upon any other scriptures that relate to this week's section of Paul's prayer?

Now that you've looked up all the words and maybe some linked scriptures, feel free to check out some commentaries that you can find on the Blue Letter Bible site or elsewhere.

Day 5

Around the campfire – as you listen to the
crackling fire, and stretch out, and look up at the
milky way visible in the cloudless sky, ponder
the treasures you've found today.

Journal your thoughts.

Day 6

Write out the section again making it personal –
either for you or for someone you're praying for.

Expand on the section with insights you've
gathered from your treasure hunt this week.

Week Three

Phil 1:10b (KJV)

10b that ye may be sincere and without offence till the day of Christ;

Day 1

Read the section in context – the entire chapter.

Look up other versions online and write out the one that you love the best. Here's a link for that: (https://www.blueletterbible.org)

Days 2&3

Look up the words in a Greek Lexicon (http://www.eliyah.com/lexicon.html)

I've **bolded** the ones that might hold amazing treasures. (Not that you're limited by my boldness.) :)

What treasures did you find? Did looking up these words make any difference in how you interpret the verses? Journal your thoughts.

Phil 1:10b that ye may be **sincere** and without **offense** till the **day** of Christ;

Day 4

Write out the entire prayer. (You can do this daily for memorization.)

Did you come upon any other scriptures that relate to this week's section of Paul's prayer?

Now that you've looked up all the words and maybe some linked scriptures, feel free to check out some commentaries that you can find on the Blue Letter Bible site or elsewhere.

Day 5

Around the campfire – as you listen to the crackling fire, and stretch out, and look up at the milky way visible in the cloudless sky, ponder the treasures you've found today.

Journal your thoughts.

Day 6

Write out the section again making it personal –
either for you or for someone you're praying for.

Expand on the section with insights you've
gathered from your treasure hunt this week.

Week Four

Phil 1:11 (KJV)

11 Being filled with the fruits of righteousness, which are by Jesus Christ, unto the glory and praise of God.

Day 1

Read the section in context – the entire chapter.

Look up other versions online and write out the one that you love the best. Here's a link for that: (https://www.blueletterbible.org)

Days 2&3

Look up the words in a Greek Lexicon (http://www.eliyah.com/lexicon.html)

I've **bolded** the ones that might hold amazing treasures. (Not that you're limited by my boldness.) :)

What treasures did you find? Did looking up these words make any difference in how you interpret the verses? Journal your thoughts.

Phil 1:11 Being **filled** with the **fruits** of **righteousness**, which are by Jesus Christ, unto the **glory** and **praise** of God.

Day 4

Write out the entire prayer. (You can do this daily for memorization.)

Did you come upon any other scriptures that relate to this week's section of Paul's prayer?

Now that you've looked up all the words and maybe some linked scriptures, feel free to check out some commentaries that you can find on the Blue Letter Bible site or elsewhere.

Day 5

Around the campfire – as you listen to the crackling fire, and stretch out, and look up at the milky way visible in the cloudless sky, ponder the treasures you've found today.

Journal your thoughts.

Day 6

Write out the section again making it personal – either for you or for someone you're praying for.

Expand on the section with insights you've gathered from your treasure hunt this week.

Section Four

Colossians 1:9b-12 (KJV)

9b For this cause we also, since the day we heard it, do not cease to pray for you, and to desire that ye might be filled with the knowledge of his will in all wisdom and spiritual understanding;
10 That ye might walk worthy of the Lord unto all pleasing, being fruitful in every good work, and increasing in the knowledge of God;
11 Strengthened with all might, according to his glorious power, unto all patience and long-suffering with joyfulness;
12 Giving thanks unto the Father, which hath made us meet to be partakers of the inheritance of the saints in light

Week One

Colossians 1:9b (KJV)

9b For this cause we also, since the day we heard it, do not cease to pray for you, and to desire that ye might be filled with the knowledge of his will in all wisdom and spiritual understanding;

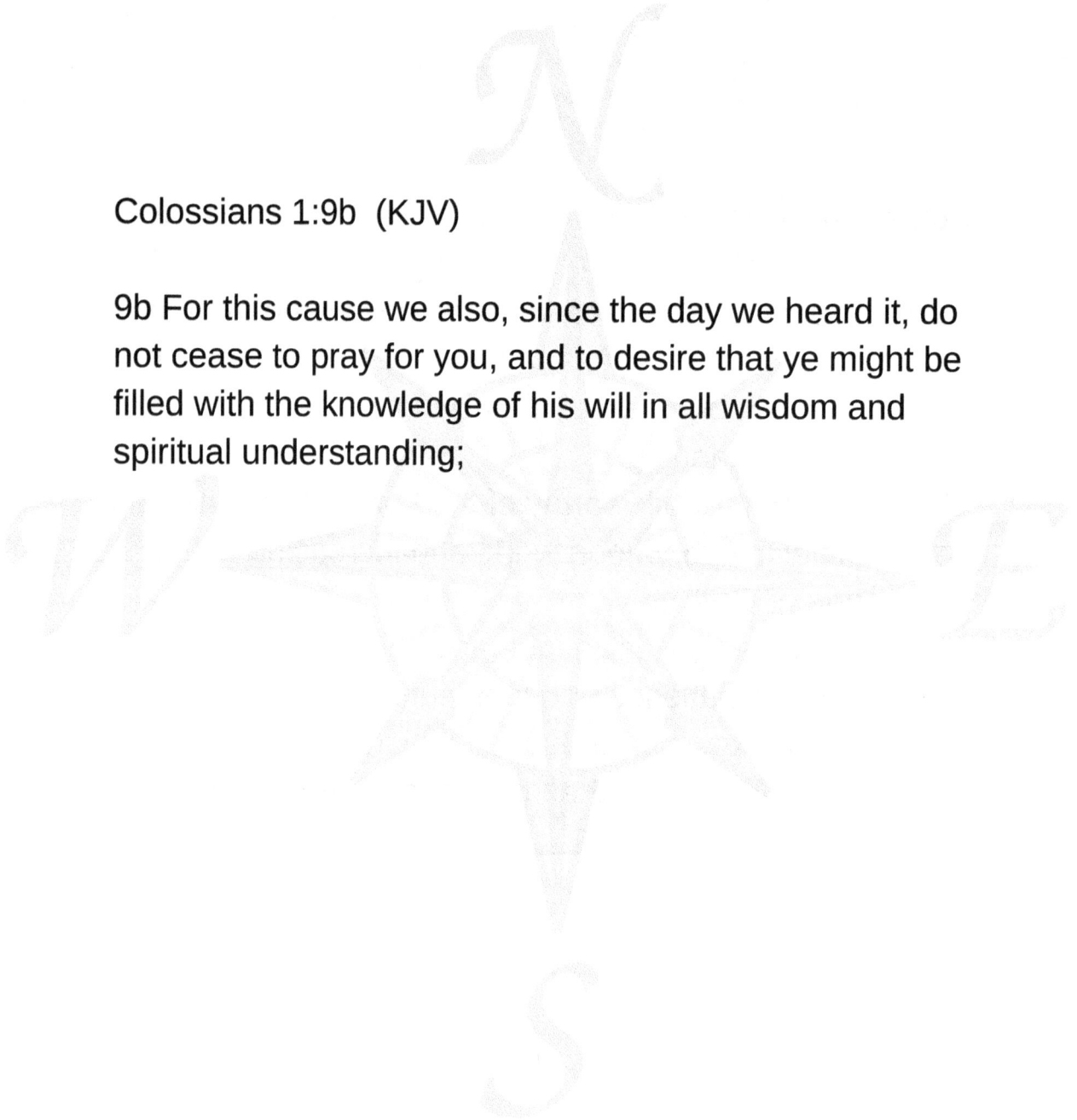

Day 1

Read the section in context – the entire chapter.

Look up other versions online and write out the one that you love the best. Here's a link for that: (https://www.blueletterbible.org)

Days 2&3

Look up the words in a Greek Lexicon (http://www.eliyah.com/lexicon.html)

I've **bolded** the ones that might hold amazing treasures. (Not that you're limited by my boldness.) :)

What treasures did you find? Did looking up these words make any difference in how you interpret the verses? Journal your thoughts.

Col 1:9b For this cause we also, since the day we heard it, **do not cease** to pray for you, and to **desire** that ye might be **filled** with the **knowledge** of his **will** in all **wisdom** and **spiritual understanding**;

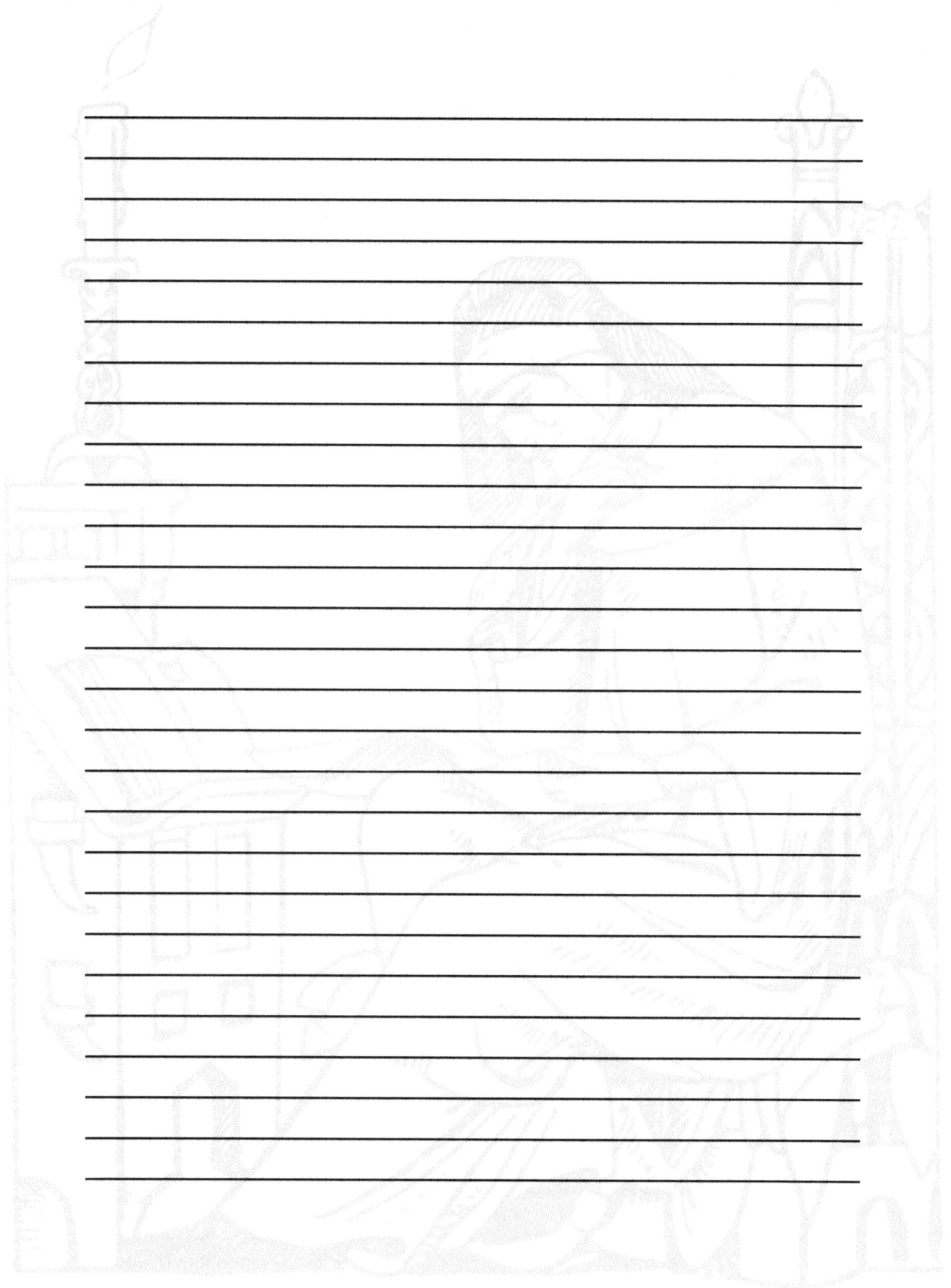

Day 4

Write out the entire prayer. (You can do this daily for memorization.)

Did you come upon any other scriptures that relate to this week's section of Paul's prayer?

Now that you've looked up all the words and maybe some linked scriptures, feel free to check out some commentaries that you can find on the Blue Letter Bible site or elsewhere.

Day 5

Around the campfire – as you listen to the crackling fire, and stretch out, and look up at the milky way visible in the cloudless sky, ponder the treasures you've found today.

Journal your thoughts.

Day 6

Write out the section again making it personal – either for you or for someone you're praying for.

Expand on the section with insights you've gathered from your treasure hunt this week.

Week Two

Colossians 1:10 (KJV)

10 That ye might walk worthy of the Lord unto all pleasing, being fruitful in every good work, and increasing in the knowledge of God;

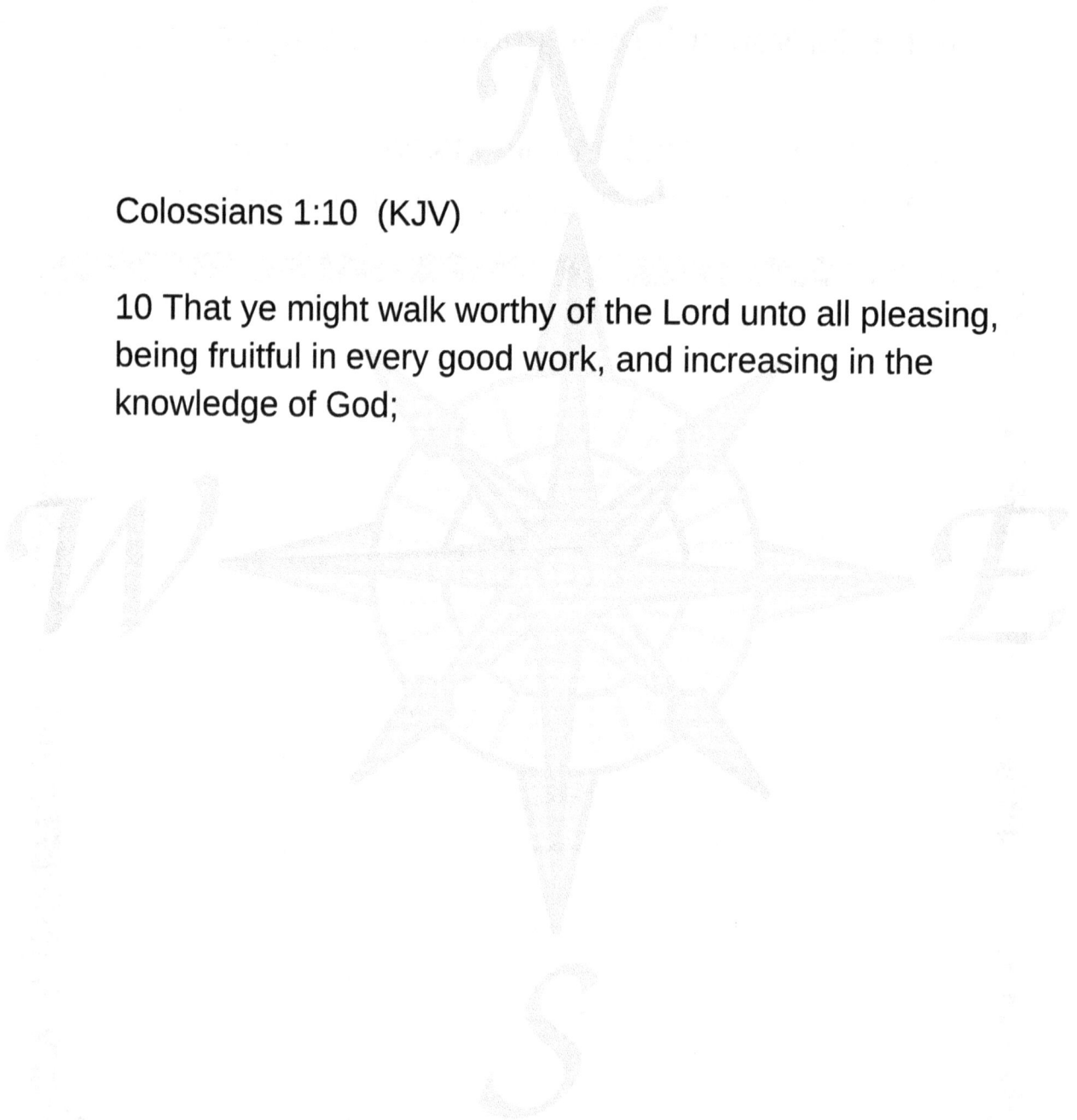

Day 1

Read the section in context – the entire chapter.

Look up other versions online and write out the one that you love the best. Here's a link for that: (https://www.blueletterbible.org)

Days 2&3

Look up the words in a Greek Lexicon (http://www.eliyah.com/lexicon.html)

I've **bolded** the ones that might hold amazing treasures. (Not that you're limited by my boldness.) :)

What treasures did you find? Did looking up these words make any difference in how you interpret the verses? Journal your thoughts.

Col 1:10 That ye might **walk worthy** of the Lord unto all **pleasing**, being **fruitful** in every **good wor**k, and **increasing** in the **knowledge** of God;

Day 4

Write out the entire prayer. (You can do this daily for memorization.)

Did you come upon any other scriptures that relate to this week's section of Paul's prayer?

Now that you've looked up all the words and maybe some linked scriptures, feel free to check out some commentaries that you can find on the Blue Letter Bible site or elsewhere.

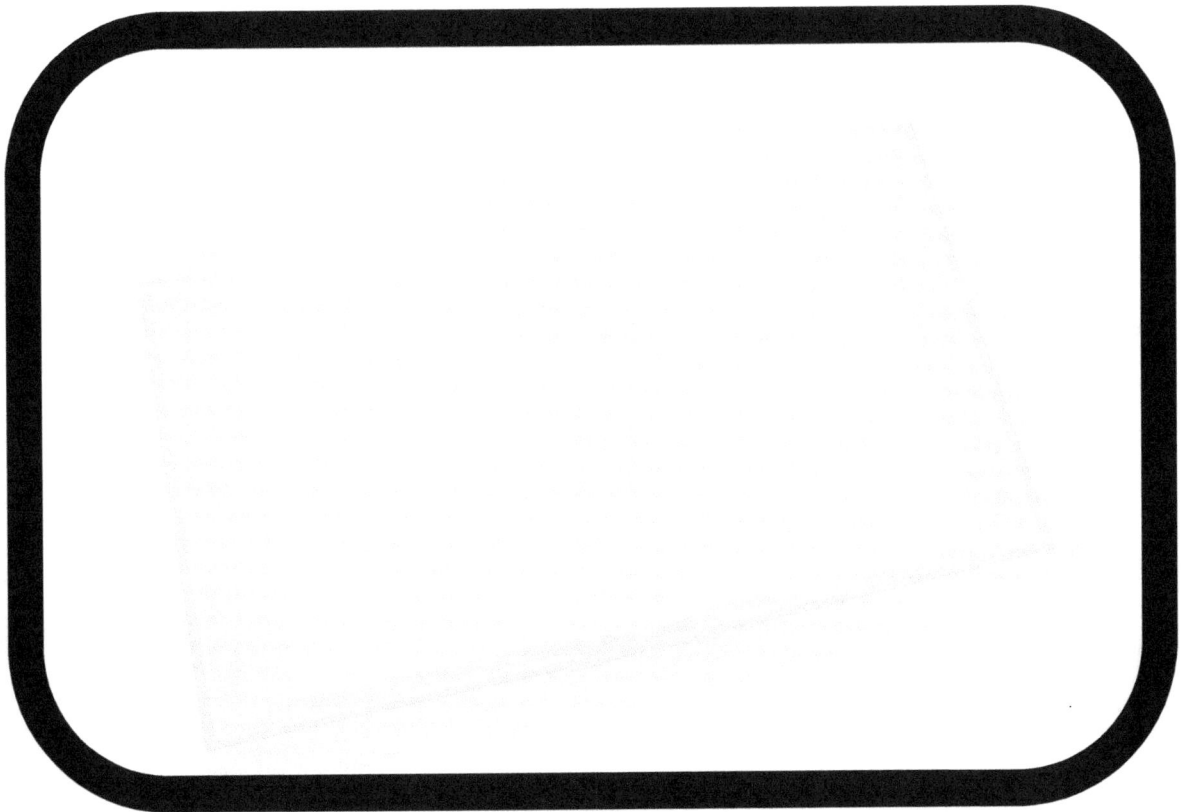

Day 5

Around the campfire – as you listen to the crackling fire, and stretch out, and look up at the milky way visible in the cloudless sky, ponder the treasures you've found today.

Journal your thoughts.

Day 6

Write out the section again making it personal – either for you or for someone you're praying for.

Expand on the section with insights you've gathered from your treasure hunt this week.

Week Three

Colossians 1:11 (KJV)

11 Strengthened with all might, according to his glorious power, unto all patience and long-suffering with joyfulness;

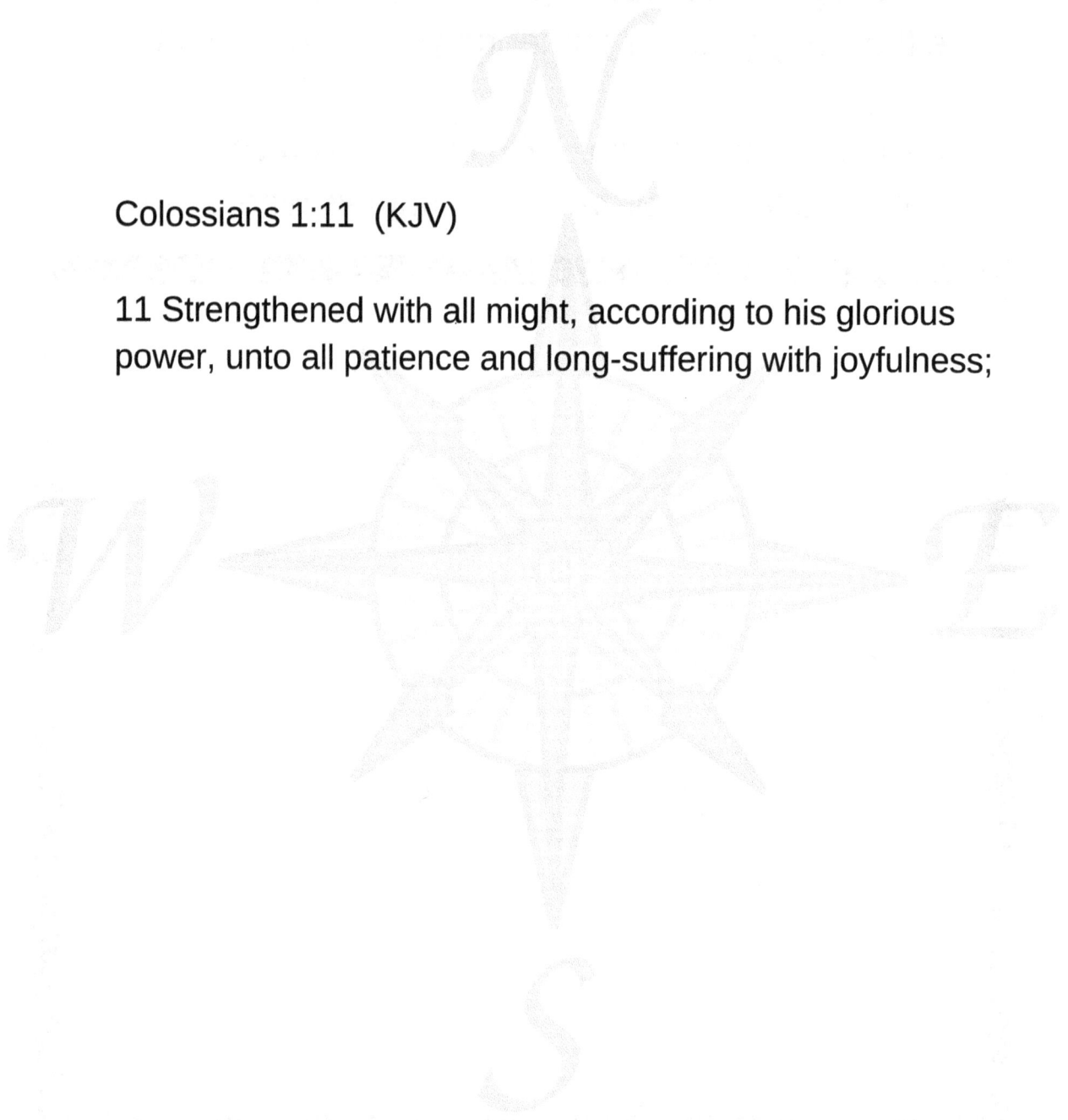

Day 1

Read the section in context – the entire chapter.

Look up other versions online and write out the one that you love the best. Here's a link for that: (https://www.blueletterbible.org)

Days 2&3

Look up the words in a Greek Lexicon (http://www.eliyah.com/lexicon.html)

I've **bolded** the ones that might hold amazing treasures. (Not that you're limited by my boldness.) :)

What treasures did you find? Did looking up these words make any difference in how you interpret the verses? Journal your thoughts.

Col 1:11 **Strengthened** with all **might**, according to his **glorious power**, unto all **patience** and **long-suffering** with **joyfulness**;

Day 4

Write out the entire prayer. (You can do this daily for memorization.)

Did you come upon any other scriptures that relate to this week's section of Paul's prayer?

Now that you've looked up all the words and maybe some linked scriptures, feel free to check out some commentaries that you can find on the Blue Letter Bible site or elsewhere.

Day 5

Around the campfire – as you listen to the
crackling fire, and stretch out, and look up at the
milky way visible in the cloudless sky, ponder
the treasures you've found today.

Journal your thoughts.

Day 6

Write out the section again making it personal – either for you or for someone you're praying for.

Expand on the section with insights you've gathered from your treasure hunt this week.

Week Four

Colossians 1:12 (KJV)

12 Giving thanks unto the Father, which hath made us meet to be partakers of the inheritance of the saints in light

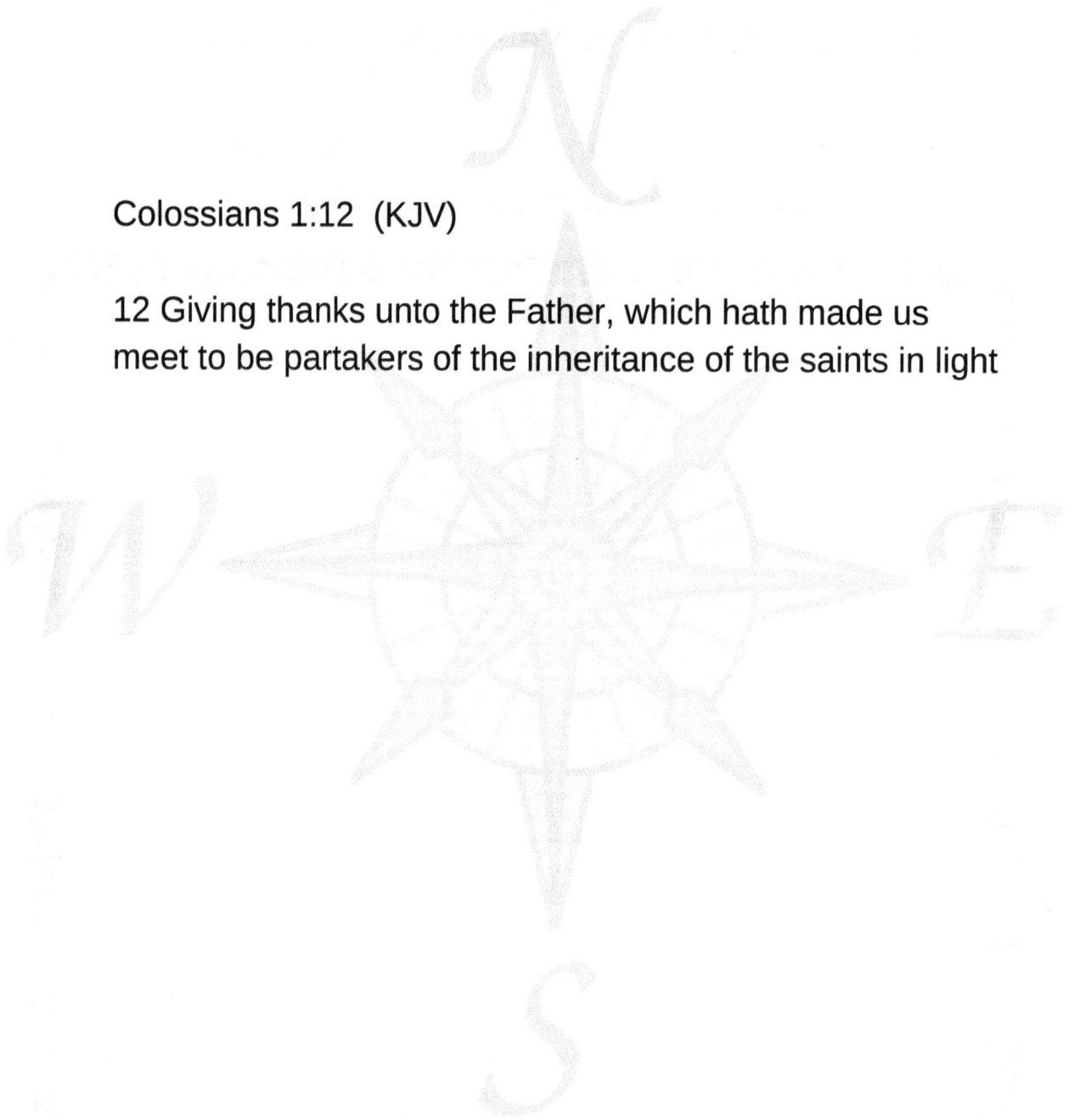

Day 1

Read the section in context – the entire chapter.

Look up other versions online and write out the one that you love the best. Here's a link for that: (https://www.blueletterbible.org)

Days 2&3

Look up the words in a Greek Lexicon
(http://www.eliyah.com/lexicon.html)

I've **bolded** the ones that might hold amazing
treasures. (Not that you're limited by my
boldness.) :)

What treasures did you find? Did looking up
these words make any difference in how you
interpret the verses? Journal your thoughts.

> Col 1:12 Giving **thanks** unto the
> Father, which hath **made** us **meet** to
> be **partakers** of the **inheritance** of
> the **saints** in **light**

Day 4

Write out the entire prayer. (You can do this daily for memorization.)

Did you come upon any other scriptures that relate to this week's section of Paul's prayer?

Now that you've looked up all the words and maybe some linked scriptures, feel free to check out some commentaries that you can find on the Blue Letter Bible site or elsewhere.

Day 5

Around the campfire – as you listen to the crackling fire, and stretch out, and look up at the milky way visible in the cloudless sky, ponder the treasures you've found today.

Journal your thoughts.

Day 6

Write out the section again making it personal – either for you or for someone you're praying for.

Expand on the section with insights you've gathered from your treasure hunt this week.

Jax Hunter is known for her heartwarming military romance series: True Heroes. She is currently writing American Revolutionary War fiction. Recently, she has ventured out to write journals: climbing trackers, motivational journals and bible study journals.

She teaches a wide variety of writing courses, both online and in person and travels the state telling the stories of April 19, 1775. She also is the owner of a health and wellness business.

Whew.

What does she do for fun? Well, she's a huge hockey fan. She has a fancy embroidery machine and she'll embroider anything that will fit in the hoop. And she collects really old books.

She lives in the high mountains of Colorado with own true hero and the two pups that rule the house.

You can find me
On Facebook
Facebook.com/writerjaxhunter
Fiction Website
JaxMHunter.com
Journal Website
byJax.com

Novels by Jax
The True Heroesl Series

Journals by Jax

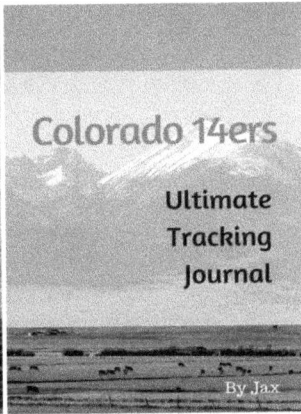

Introducing
the Dig Deep
in Scripture
Series

Collect
them all!

Coming Soon

www.ingramcontent.com/pod-product-compliance
Lightning Source LLC
LaVergne TN
LVHW061305060426
835513LV00013B/1249